The Wise Writer's

Workbook

PLAN   CREATE   SAVE   FIND

Anna Questerly

ISBN-13: 978-1987408843

ISBN-10:1987408845

For information about permission to reproduce selections from this book, send an email to AnnaQuesterly@gmail.com with "Permissions" in the subject line.

For information about having Anna Questerly speak to your group, school, conference, or workshop, send an email line to AnnaQuesterly@gmail.com with "Request for Speaking Engagement" in the subject line.

For information about special discounts on bulk purchases, send an email to AnnaQuesterly@gmail.com with "Bulk Purchases: in the subject line.

Project Information

Working Title:

Genre/Subject:

Estimated Word Count:

Target Reader:

Inciting Idea:

Blockbuster Premise:

Started:

Finished:

Published:

Notes:

Acknowledgements

There are so many people to thank for the development and creation of this workbook. From the wonderful members of Romance Writers of America, and all of the authors who have visited Dog-Eared Pages bookstore, to the many authors I have met throughout the past decade at events, conferences, and workshops who have so generously shared their hints, tips, tricks, mistakes, quirks, frustrations, and knowledge, I say...

& a special thank you to my beta-reading team who took the time to help me make this particular book better than I had originally imagined. You guys are the best! Duann Black, Charles L.M. Plumb, Nelle Lewis, and Michele Venné thank you so much. Hugs to all!

And I will always be grateful to have Thom in my life. He always makes sure I have the best support system for everything I do. Kisses, baby!

Table of Contents

Table of Contents continued

If necessity is the mother of invention, chaos must be the father. I know a few writers, and it *is* possible one or two of them are highly organized beings who keep orderly records and color-coded files, backed up in triplicate on three different devices, and stored in the cloud. I don't. Not even close.

No, I'm one of those writers who scribble on post-its and scrawl in the margins of notebooks. While I'm working on a project, piles of scrap paper litter my desk, the dining room table, and the tops of the file cabinet. Timelines, maps, and sketches are tacked to the wall. Character sheets are spread across my desk, and a scene outline sits beside my laptop. All of this is quite handy when I'm writing from home, not so much when I'm away.

Plus, once I finish a project I have no idea what happens to all of my notes – they simply vanish. I'm certain I put them somewhere safe…

This was a major problem when I decided to continue my *Minstrel's Tale* trilogy. I have to recreate all of my characters' back stories, my maps, timelines all of it. It's not as simple as reading through it again. What color were Lissette's eyes? How many children did Jonathan have? How much did I tell about Edrea? The answer to each was available by rereading the book, of course, but every time I had a new question, I had to reread again. There had to be a more efficient way to keep my stories straight. Right?

I'd heard of organization programs for writers. I even downloaded one to my phone – once. After the first few fumbling entries, I never opened that app again. As far as trying to use technology for staying organized while writing, the closest I got was to sometimes jot myself an email and then promptly forget where I saved it.

So I asked around and learned a few of my writer friends use Scrivener, and they really like it. But I'm not one to sit in front of a keyboard when plotting and scheming. I like to kick back, pencil in hand, and figure these things out. When I'm in front of the keyboard, I'm writing.

What I needed was a scribbler's version of Scrivener. This is what you're now holding in your hand. From the Character Development Sheets to the Self-Publishing Checklist, I encourage you to fill the following pages with your fictional worlds and discover a convenient way to keep your own story straight.

I have incorporated as many useful tools, tips, and functional pages, while leaving enough room for you to add your own guidelines, gadgets, and gizmos. Some writers may use this as a planner for their first novel, while others will find it a handy storage medium for those troublesome details needed for that crucial credible continuity in a series we all strive to maintain.

As a creative person by nature, I bet you'll find even more ways to use this workbook than I've included. My beta-readers certainly did. I added the Timeline pages because I write historical fiction and needed to keep my fictional timeline in line with history. But one of my beta-readers plans to use separate Timeline pages for each main character, and another will use them for tracking subplots in relation to the main plot. Brilliant!

The same thing happened with the Calendar pages: a few plan to use them for a production schedule and others for marketing plans, and yet I had included them as a way to track word count and writing goals.

Also, because of another suggestion, I added a Notes page to the *backs* of the functional pages (Maps, Timeline, and Storyboard pages). This small change enables writers to remove those pages and tape them to the wall if they so choose. Otherwise, had I printed on both the front and back, they may have lost the use of half of the functional pages. However, for the writer who prefers to use the book intact, the suggestion of adding one additional Notes page *before* these functional pages, saves writer's from flipping back and forth to add notes to the back of the page, as now the Notes page and the functional page are facing each other.

This type of feedback is why beta-readers are so important. As I mentioned earlier, each of them have my gratitude for their honest evaluation and invaluable feedback. By the way, page 151 helps to keep track of those feisty folks, too.

I think most of the workbook is self-explanatory. I added a few notes here and there, as much for my own benefit as to assist new writers. Those of you, who don't need the plot points explained or perhaps use a different story structure, please feel free to skip pages or change things as you see fit.

Go ahead Wise Writer – it's your workbook now. Take ownership. Use a Sharpie to write **your** project name on the spine and on the front cover. Have fun with it! If you think of additional features you'd like to see in a future edition, drop me a line at AnnaQuesterly@gmail.com. Your suggestion might be included next time.

Keep on writin'

P.S. If you do find the *Wise Writer's Workbook* helpful, I hope you will consider leaving a great review online and telling your writing friends about it. Much appreciated!

Character Archive

In this chapter, you'll find worksheets to help you:

- ➢ Create and develop believable:
  - ➢ Main/Primary Characters
    - Hero
    - Heroine
    - Villain
  - ➢ Secondary Characters
    - Sidekicks or Partners
    - Close Friends
    - Immediate Family
  - ➢ Minor/Tertiary Characters
- ➢ Maintain character continuity
- ➢ Fully explore your characters
- ➢ Build and develop relationships
- ➢ Create a character arc for each main character

"I don't know where people got the idea that characters in books are supposed to be likable. Books are not in the business of creating merely likeable characters with whom you can have some simple identification with. Books are in the business of creating great stories that make your brain go ahhbdgbdmerhbergurhbudgerbudbaaarr."

— John Green

Character Tips & Tricks Learned

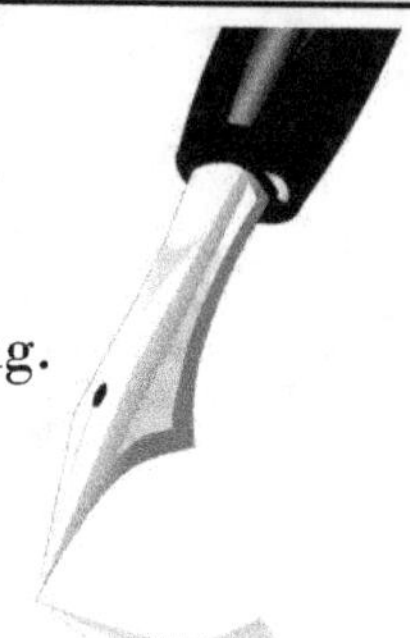

Use this section for important notes on character building.

Notes:

Character Relationship Tree

Write character names or action verbs inside as many frames as you need to show relationships between characters. **Pro Tip: Add page numbers *in pencil* when a character first appears in your manuscript.**

Use the following pages to build your characters and to remember their traits for your next book!

Pro Tip: Don't forget to use your character's Action Verbs!

Main Characters

Name:

Nickname:

Age: Gender: Race: Religion:

Profession: Social Class:

Transportation:

Appearance:

Strengths/Abilities:

Fears/Dislikes:

Likes/Hobbies:

Habits/Tics/Quirks:

Items in wallet/purse:

Items in closet:

Favorite Songs/Movies/Books:

Friends/Relatives:

Enemies:

Synonyms for
Action Verb:

History:

Goals:

Motivation:

Conflict:

Metaphors/Similes:

Main Characters

Action Verb:

Name: Items in wallet/purse:

Nickname:

Age: Gender: Race: Religion:

Profession: Social Class:

Transportation:

Appearance:

Items in closet:

Strengths/Abilities:

Fears/Dislikes: Favorite Songs/Movies/Books:

Likes/Hobbies: Friends/Relatives:

Habits/Tics/Quirks:

Enemies:

Synonyms for
Action Verb:

History:

Goals:

Motivation:

Conflict:

Metaphors/Similes:

Main Characters

Action Verb:

Name:

Nickname:

Age: Gender: Race: Religion:

Profession: Social Class:

Transportation:

Appearance:

Strengths/Abilities:

Fears/Dislikes:

Likes/Hobbies:

Habits/Tics/Quirks:

Items in wallet/purse:

Items in closet:

Favorite Songs/Movies/Books:

Friends/Relatives:

Enemies:

Synonyms for
Action Verb:

History:

Goals:

Motivation:

Conflict:

Metaphors/Similes:

Main Characters

Action Verb:

Name:

Nickname:

Age: Gender: Race: Religion:

Profession: Social Class:

Transportation:

Appearance:

Strengths/Abilities:

Fears/Dislikes:

Likes/Hobbies:

Habits/Tics/Quirks:

Items in wallet/purse:

Items in closet:

Favorite Songs/Movies/Books:

Friends/Relatives:

Enemies:

Synonyms for
Action Verb:

History:

Goals:

Motivation:

Conflict:

Metaphors/Similes:

Main Characters

Action Verb:

Name:

Nickname:

Age: Gender: Race: Religion:

Profession: Social Class:

Transportation:

Appearance:

Strengths/Abilities:

Fears/Dislikes:

Likes/Hobbies:

Habits/Tics/Quirks:

Items in wallet/purse:

Items in closet:

Favorite Songs/Movies/Books:

Friends/Relatives:

Enemies:

Synonyms for
Action Verb:

History:

Goals:

Motivation:

Conflict:

Metaphors/Similes:

Action Verb:

Name: Nickname:

Age: Gender: Race: Religion:

Profession: Social Class:

Relationship to the main character:

Appearance:

Strengths/Abilities:

Fears/Dislikes:

Transportation:

History:

Goals: Motivation:

Items in wallet/purse:

Items in closet:

Friends/Relatives/Enemies:

Synonyms for Action Verb:

Conflict:

Action Verb: **Secondary Characters**

Name: Nickname: Items in wallet/purse:

Age: Gender: Race: Religion:

Profession: Social Class:

Relationship to the main character: Items in closet:

Appearance:

Friends/Relatives/Enemies:

Strengths/Abilities:

Synonyms for Action Verb:

Fears/Dislikes:

Transportation:

History:

Goals: Motivation: Conflict:

Action Verb:

Name: Nickname:

Items in wallet/purse:

Age: Gender: Race: Religion:

Profession: Social Class:

Relationship to the main character:

Items in closet:

Appearance:

Friends/Relatives/Enemies:

Strengths/Abilities:

Synonyms for Action Verb:

Fears/Dislikes:

Transportation:

History:

Goals: Motivation: Conflict:

Action Verb:

Secondary Characters

Name: Nickname: Items in wallet/purse:

Age: Gender: Race: Religion:

Profession: Social Class:

Relationship to the main character: Items in closet:

Appearance:

Friends/Relatives/Enemies:

Strengths/Abilities:

Synonyms for Action Verb:

Fears/Dislikes:

Transportation:

History:

Goals: Motivation: Conflict:

Action Verb:

Name: Nickname:

Items in wallet/purse:

Age: Gender: Race: Religion:

Profession: Social Class:

Relationship to the main character:

Items in closet:

Appearance:

Friends/Relatives/Enemies:

Strengths/Abilities:

Synonyms for Action Verb:

Fears/Dislikes:

Transportation:

History:

Goals: Motivation: Conflict:

Action Verb: **Secondary Characters**

Name: Nickname: Items in wallet/purse:

Age: Gender: Race: Religion:

Profession: Social Class:

Relationship to the main character: Items in closet:

Appearance:

                                                                   Friends/Relatives/Enemies:

Strengths/Abilities:

                                                                   Synonyms for Action Verb:

Fears/Dislikes:

Transportation:

History:

Goals: Motivation: Conflict:

Action Verb:

Name: Nickname:

Items in wallet/purse:

Age: Gender: Race: Religion:

Profession: Social Class:

Relationship to the main character:

Items in closet:

Appearance:

Friends/Relatives/Enemies:

Strengths/Abilities:

Synonyms for Action Verb:

Fears/Dislikes:

Transportation:

History:

Goals: Motivation: Conflict:

Action Verb: **Secondary Characters**

Name: Nickname: Items in wallet/purse:

Age: Gender: Race: Religion:

Profession: Social Class:

Relationship to the main character: Items in closet:

Appearance:

Friends/Relatives/Enemies:

Strengths/Abilities:

Synonyms for Action Verb:

Fears/Dislikes:

Transportation:

History:

Goals: Motivation: Conflict:

Action Verb:

Name: Nickname:

Items in wallet/purse:

Age: Gender: Race: Religion:

Profession: Social Class:

Relationship to the main character:

Items in closet:

Appearance:

Friends/Relatives/Enemies:

Strengths/Abilities:

Synonyms for Action Verb:

Fears/Dislikes:

Transportation:

History:

Goals: Motivation: Conflict:

Action Verb:

Secondary Characters

Name: Nickname: Items in wallet/purse:

Age: Gender: Race: Religion:

Profession: Social Class:

Relationship to the main character: Items in closet:

Appearance:

Friends/Relatives/Enemies:

Strengths/Abilities:

Synonyms for Action Verb:

Fears/Dislikes:

Transportation:

History:

Goals: Motivation: Conflict:

Action Verb:

Name: Nickname:

Items in wallet/purse:

Age: Gender: Race: Religion:

Profession: Social Class:

Relationship to the main character:

Items in closet:

Appearance:

Friends/Relatives/Enemies:

Strengths/Abilities:

Synonyms for Action Verb:

Fears/Dislikes:

Transportation:

History:

Goals: Motivation: Conflict:

Action Verb:

Secondary Characters

Items in wallet/purse:

Name: Nickname:

Age: Gender: Race: Religion:

Profession: Social Class:

Items in closet:

Relationship to the main character:

Appearance:

Friends/Relatives/Enemies:

Strengths/Abilities:

Synonyms for Action Verb:

Fears/Dislikes:

Transportation:

History:

Goals: Motivation: Conflict:

Action Verb:

Name: Nickname:

Items in wallet/purse:

Age: Gender: Race: Religion:

Profession: Social Class:

Relationship to the main character:

Items in closet:

Appearance:

Friends/Relatives/Enemies:

Strengths/Abilities:

Synonyms for Action Verb:

Fears/Dislikes:

Transportation:

History:

Goals: Motivation: Conflict:

Action Verb:

Secondary Characters

Name: Nickname: Items in wallet/purse:

Age: Gender: Race: Religion:

Profession: Social Class:

Relationship to the main character: Items in closet:

Appearance:

Friends/Relatives/Enemies:

Strengths/Abilities:

Synonyms for Action Verb:

Fears/Dislikes:

Transportation:

History:

Goals: Motivation: Conflict:

Minor/Tertiary Characters

Action Verb:

Name:

Age: Gender: Profession:

Appearance:

Notes:

Action Verb:

Name:

Age: Gender: Profession:

Appearance:

Notes:

Action Verb:

Name:

Age: Gender: Profession:

Appearance:

Notes:

Action Verb:

Name:

Age: Gender: Profession:

Appearance:

Notes:

Action Verb:

Name:

Age: Gender: Profession:

Appearance:

Notes:

Action Verb:

Name:

Age: Gender: Profession:

Appearance:

Notes:

Minor/Tertiary Characters

Action Verb:

Name:

Age: Gender: Profession:

Appearance:

Notes:

Action Verb:

Name:

Age: Gender: Profession:

Appearance:

Notes:

Action Verb:

Name:

Age: Gender: Profession:

Appearance:

Notes:

Action Verb:

Name:

Age: Gender: Profession:

Appearance:

Notes:

Action Verb:

Name:

Age: Gender: Profession:

Appearance:

Notes:

Action Verb:

Name:

Age: Gender: Profession:

Appearance:

Notes:

Notes:

Notes:

Notes:

Notes:

Plot Blueprint

In this chapter, you'll find tools and worksheets to help you:

- ➤ Identify Plot Points aka Beat Sheet
- ➤ Craft Tagline & Elevator Pitch
- ➤ Craft Back Cover Copy
- ➤ Create Storyboards for
    - Organizing Chapters
    - Making Notes for Scenes
    - Outlining Chapters
- ➤ Develop a Scene List

"Plot is no more than footprints left in the snow after your characters have run by on their way to incredible destinations."

— Ray Bradbury, *Zen in the Art of Writing*

Plot Tips & Tricks Learned

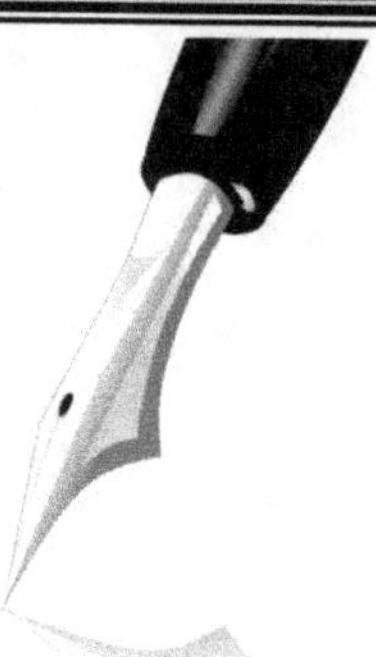

Use this section for important notes on plot and story arc.

Notes:

Plot Points aka Beat Sheet

Act I

Opening Hook – A scene to hook the reader and introduce main character(s). The hook should give a glimpse as to the conflict and set the tone of the story.

Set Up – In this scene, give the reader a little more information on the present world of your hero. Make sure to show your character's main weakness. This scene establishes what your story is really about and how your character will change throughout. Also known as the Character Redemption Arc.

Inciting Incident – Also known as the Call-To-Action. This is where the adventure starts. Show the reader who/what is forcing your heroine to take action.

Plot Point 1 – Everyone has doubts or fear. What is holding your character back? What must he overcome to face the journey ahead?

Save the Cat – This tip is from the book *Save the Cat* by Blake Snyder. At some point in the First Act, try to show some good in your character, give us some reason to like her, even if she appears completely flawed in the beginning.

Act II

The Choice – This is the time to show your main character actively choosing to move forward and the adventure begins.

Subplot – Many times the subplot underscores the main theme. For example, if your novel's main theme is trust, your subplot might show doubt and wariness.

Game On! – Your hero gathers clues, explores this world, tries and fails several times to find the treasure, kill the bad guy, etc. Generally, at this point your story is living up to its hype and the promises from the front and back covers of the book.

Pinch 1 – The pinch scenes are where pressure is applied to your characters, forcing them onward. It's also showcases the seriousness of the threat and outlines the stakes.

Midpoint – Think of this as an early ending that will be the opposite of the actual ending. For example, the hero captures the killer, but later we find out it's the wrong guy. Or the heroine creates a spell to keep her safe and only *later finds out about the side effects. Usually a case of be careful what you ask for.

Pinch 2 – Another scene tied to Pinch 1 reminding readers of the central conflict, and applies more pressure to your character(s).

***OOPS!** – This is the *later mentioned in the Midpoint, when the character first begins to realize their mistake. Not only do fear and doubt plague the hero, but the bad guys are most likely after him, too.

Kill the Dog – The moment when the heroine realizes she's lost everything she thought she'd gained or that none of it even matters anymore. Her goal no longer seems possible. Many times a beloved character dies or at the very least there is an emotional death. This is the part of the story where we want the reader to weep. (Think *Marley and Me*, *Old Yeller*, *Sounder*, etc.)

Plot Point 2 or **The Black Moment** – Killing the Dog was the last straw. Now, our hero is finished. He's lost. He sees no path forward and his entire quest seems hopeless.

Act III

Aha! Moment – A sudden realization or possible subplot assistance gives our heroine a second chance to reach her goal. She picks herself up, dusts herself off, and goes at it again.

Showdown! – Using all he's learned from earlier attempts and what he now knows about himself, our hero finally has the experience to achieve his goal. The conflict is resolved and the theme of the story holds true.

Dénouement – Wrap it up. Have the heroine ride into the sunset. Everyone lives happily ever after. For a more rewarding ending, tie it all up by showing the character's growth in relation to how we met her at the opening scene – bringing it full circle.

THE END

Act I

Opening
Hook:

Setup:

Inciting Incident:

Plot Point 1:

The Choice:

Subplot:

Game On!

Pinch 1:

Midpoint:

Pinch 2:

OOPS!

Kill the Dog:

Plot Point 2 or The Black Moment:

Act III

Aha!
Moment:

Showdown:

Denoument:

Tagline & Elevator Pitch Worksheet

Figure about 20-30 seconds maximum speaking time. Average speaking speed is 150 words per minute, which is about 50-75 words maximum. Try out a few options below.

Try out a few Taglines below.

Try to keep them at less than 12 words.

Back Cover Copy

Jot down a few ideas below. Average range for back cover copy is 150-200 words. Again, don't forget to use as many Power Words as possible.

Notes:

Notes:

Notes:

Notes:

Notes:

Notes:

Notes:

Notes:

Notes:

Notes:

1.
2.
3.
4.
5.
6.
7.
8.
9.
10.
11.
12.
13.
14.
15.
16.
17.
18.
19.
20.
21.
22.
23.
24.
25.
26.
27.
28.
29.
30.
31.
32.
33.
34.
35.

36.
37.
38.
39.
40.
41.
42.
43.
44.
45.
46.
47.
48.
49.
50.
51.
52.
53.
54.
55.
56.
57.
58.
59.
60.
61.
62.
63.
64.
65.
66.
67.
68.
69.
70.

Elements of Setting

In this chapter, you'll find worksheets to help you:

- ➤ Build Fictional Worlds
- ➤ Sketch Maps and Landmarks
- ➤ Create Realistic Settings
- ➤ Use Setting to Evoke Specific Mood/Ambiance
- ➤ Create and Track Timelines
  - Use one per character or
  - Use separate ones for plots and subplots or
  - Use to ensure real world/fictional world continuity in historical fiction.

"Every story would be another story, and unrecognizable if it took up its characters and plot and happened somewhere else... Fiction depends for its life on place. Place is the crossroads of circumstance, the proving ground of, What happened? Who's here? Who's coming?...."

— Eudora Welty

Setting Tips & Tricks Learned

Use this section for important notes on world-building.

Notes:

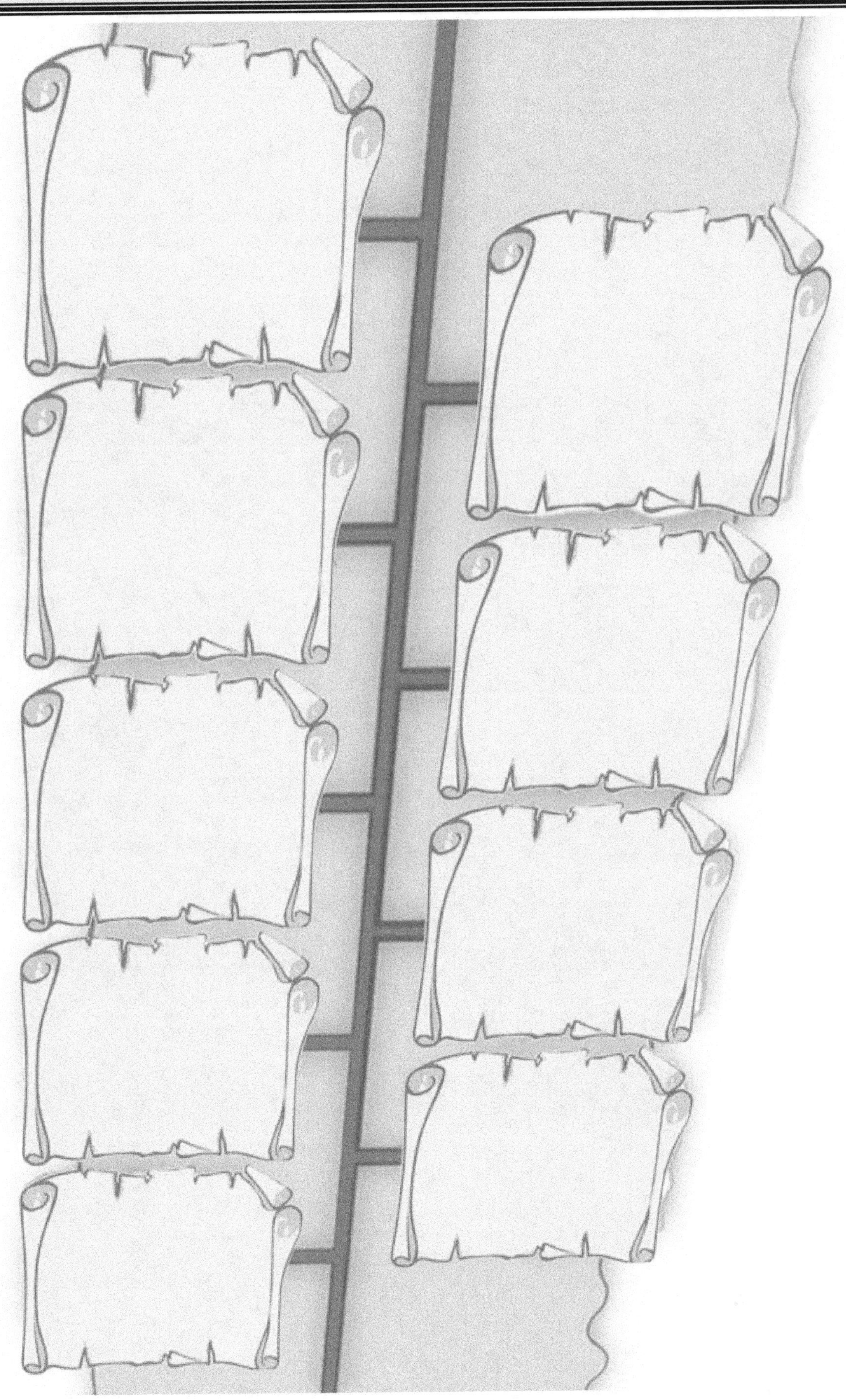

Notes:

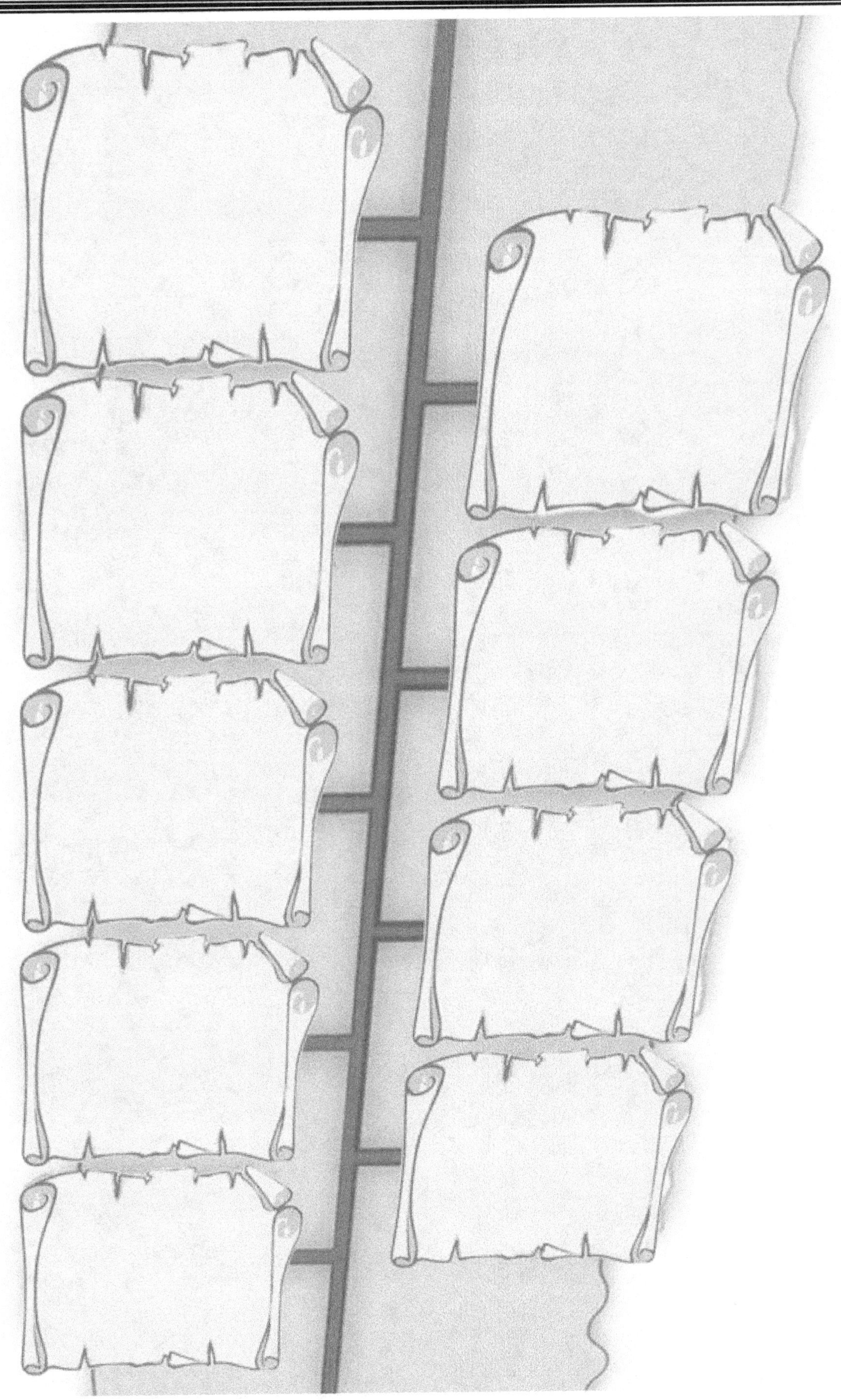

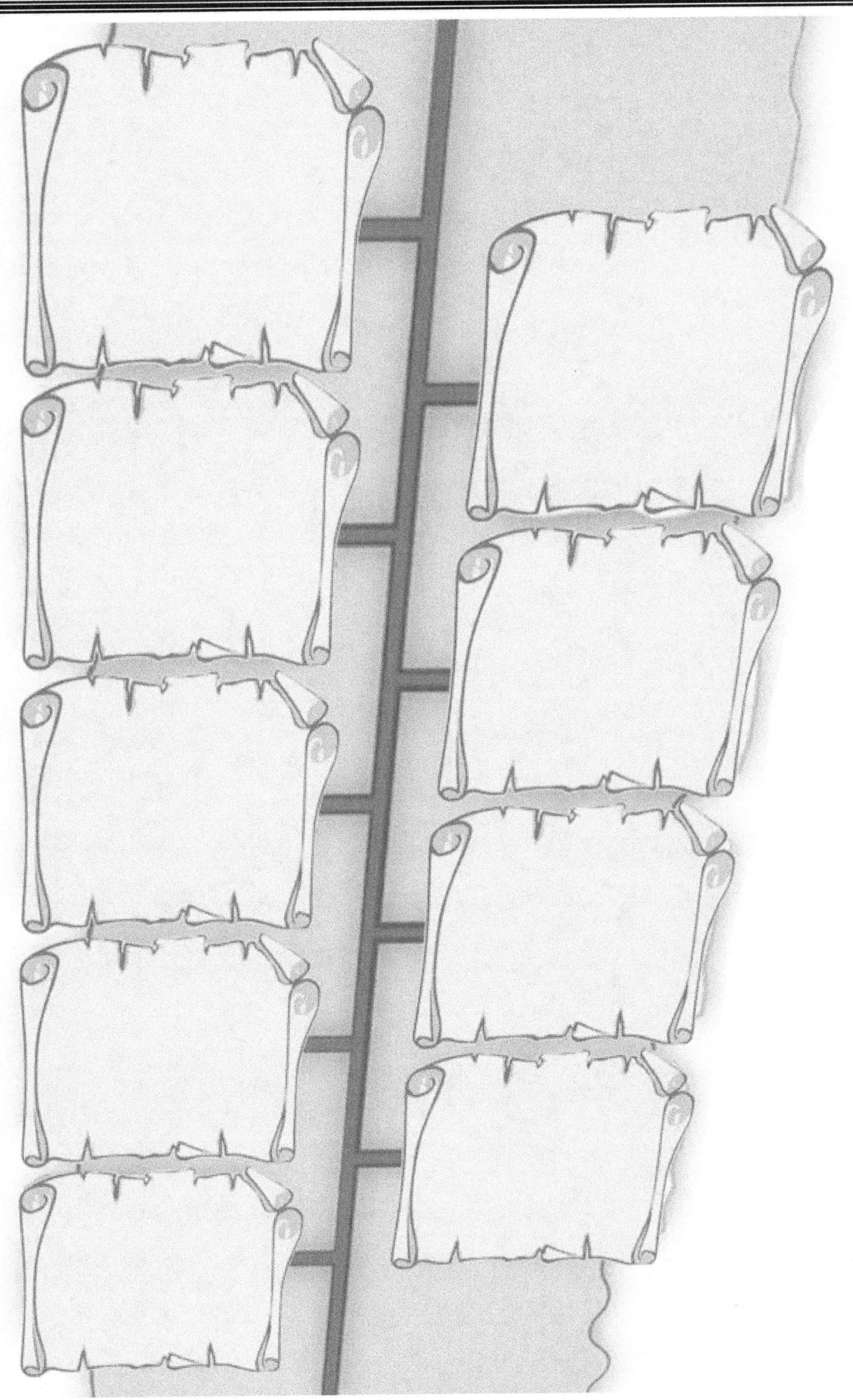

Notes:

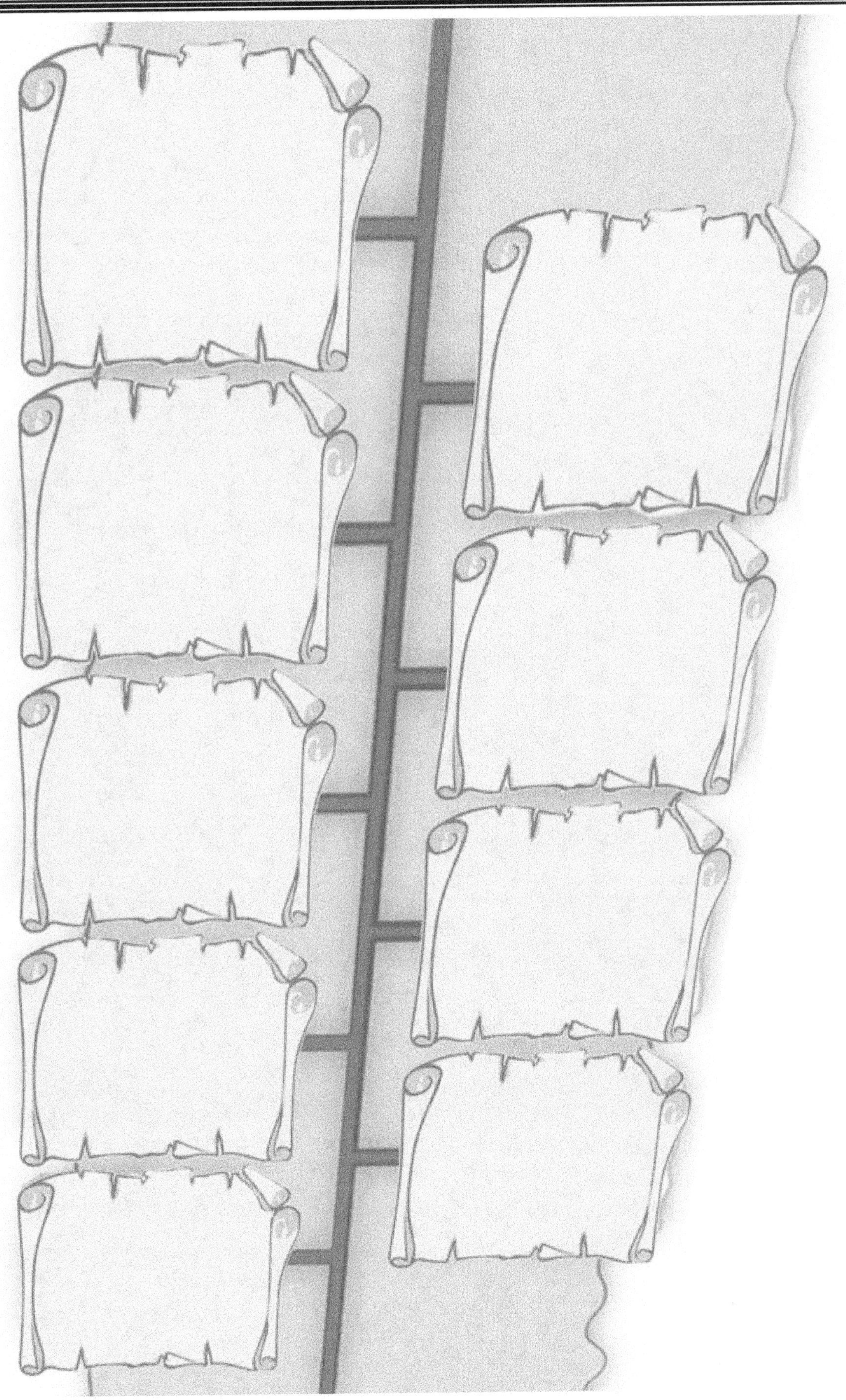

Notes:

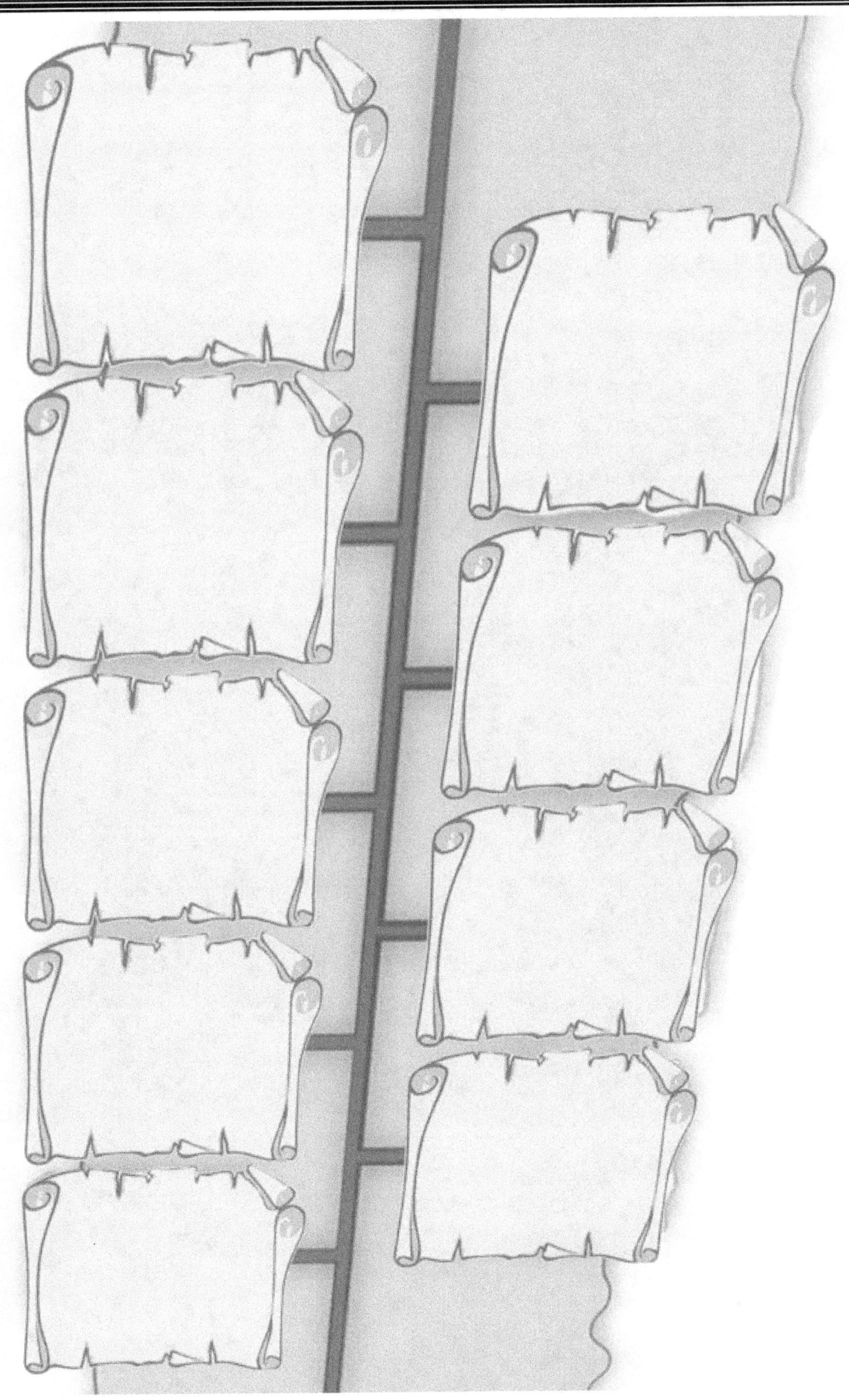

Notes:

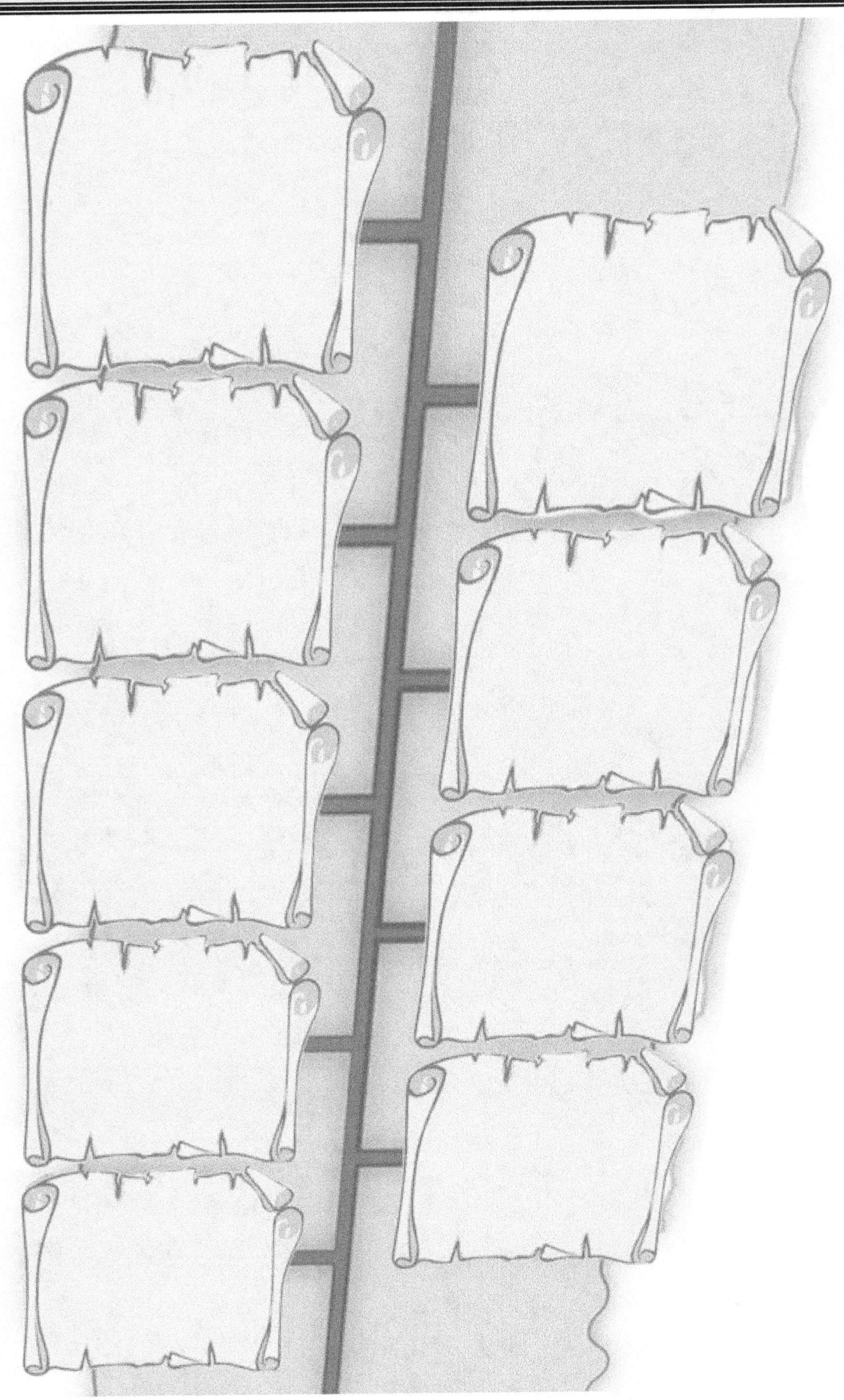

Notes:

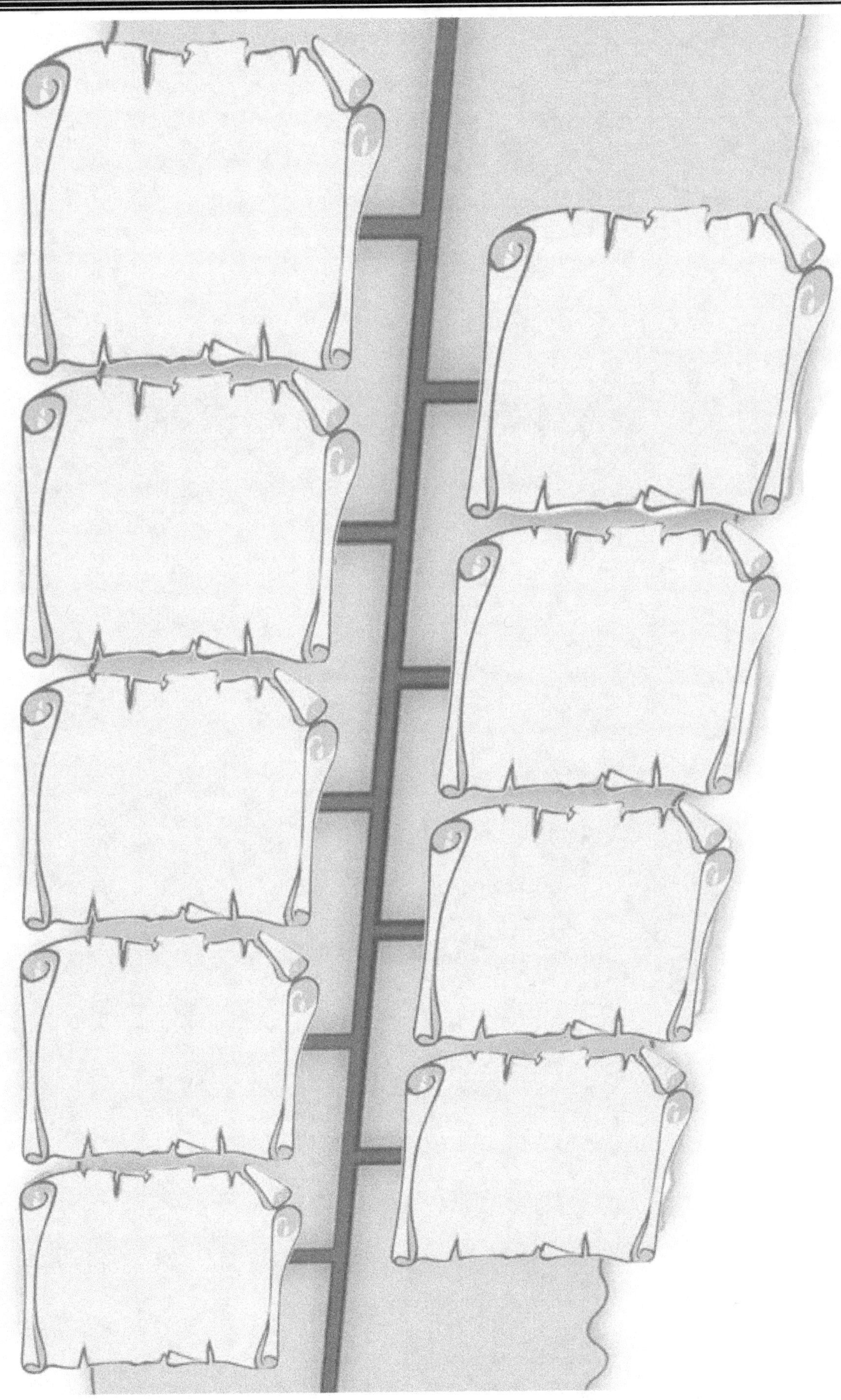

Notes:

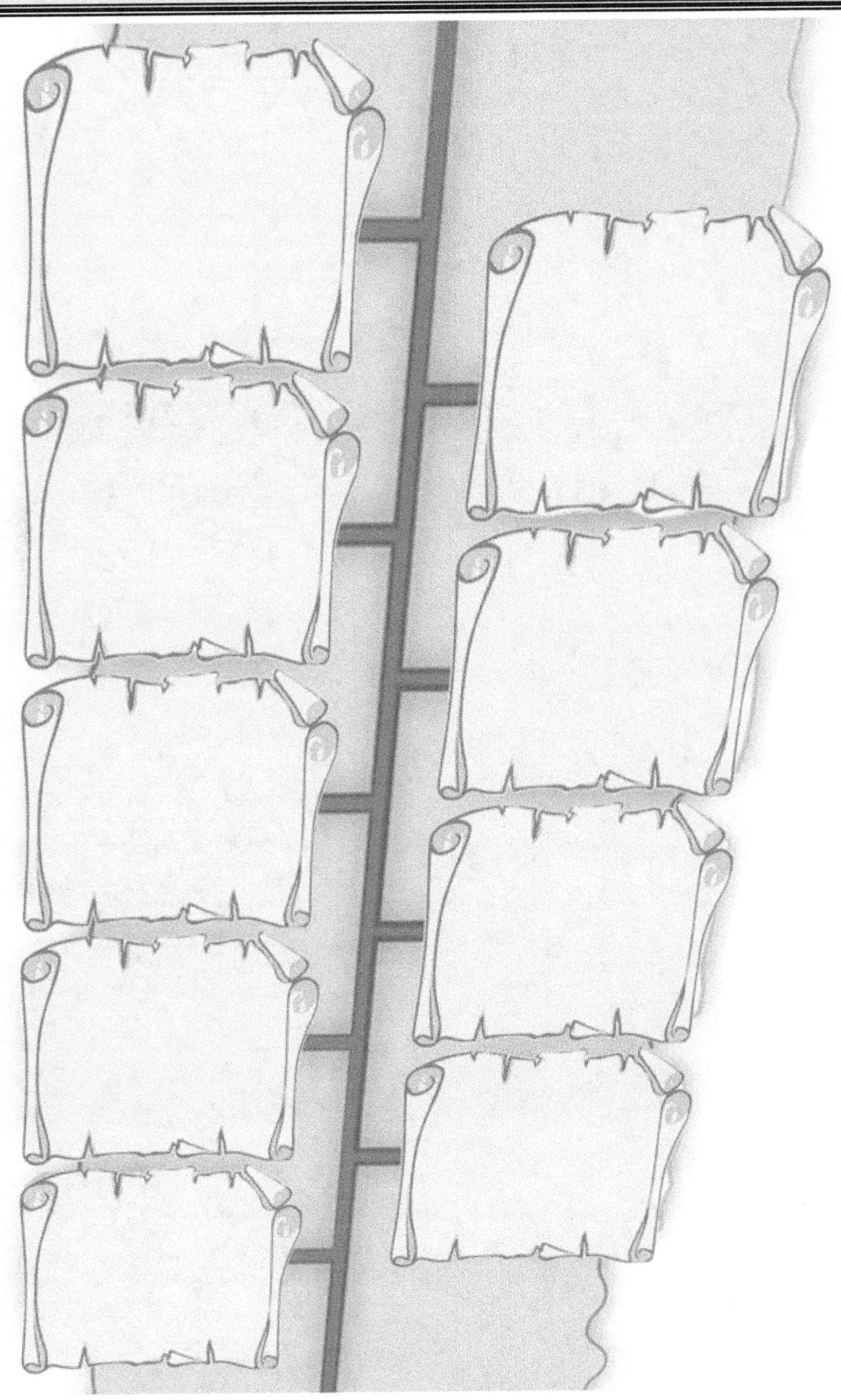

Notes:

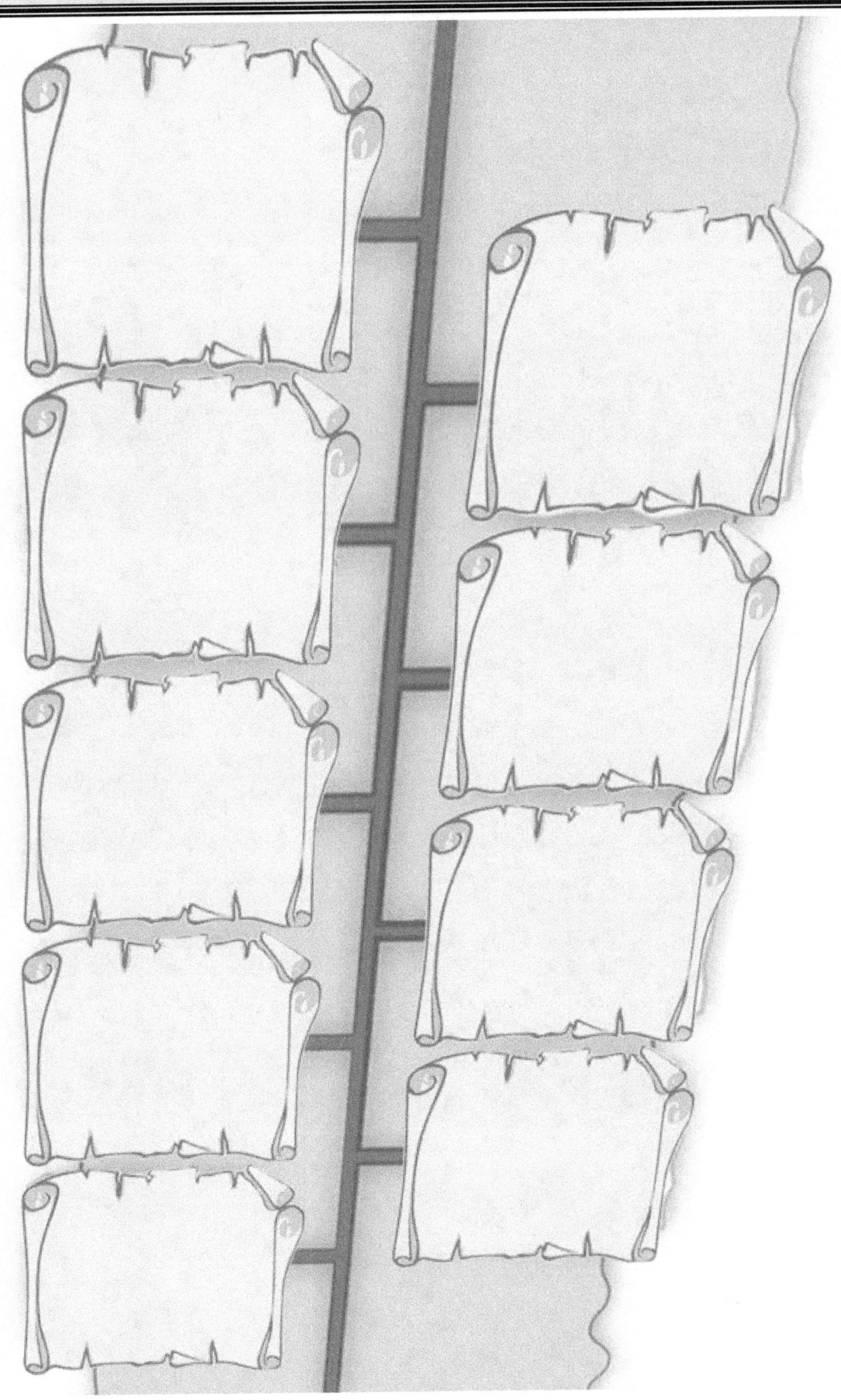

Notes:

Setting and World-Building Notes

Historical
Information:

Ancestral
Influences:

Setting and World-Building Notes

Resources:

Setting and World-Building Notes

Social
Enviorment:

Cultural
Environment:

Political
Environment:

Religious
Environment:

Setting and World-Building Notes

Time Span of Story:

Time of Year:

Climate:

Mood/Ambiance:

**Thematic
Elements:**

Topographical Maps and Sketches

Topographical Maps and Sketches

Notes:

Topographical Maps and Sketches

Notes:

Word Clouds

Creative Cues for:

- ➢ Colors
- ➢ Descriptors
- ➢ Lazy Words
- ➢ Active Verbs

"The difference between the almost right word and the right word is really a large matter. 'tis the difference between the lightning bug and the lightning."
— Mark Twain

Pro tip: Use the following pages to spark ideas for unique & interesting word choices!

brunette
amber
honey
spice
taupe
pecan
cider
walnut
ochre
gingerbread
copper
espresso
BROWN
caramel
carob
beaver
beige
bronze
cedar
tea
khaki
sienna
coffee
tortilla
auburn
peanut
chestnut
tan
cocoa
camel
syrup
russet
mocha
sand
hickory
coyote
umber
lion
fallow
chicory
mahogany
liver
penny
sepia
clay
chocolate
buff
fawn
tawny

crocodile
hunter
kelly
seafoam
pear
green-apple
moss
asparagus
honeydew
spring
pistachio
dollar-bill
cyan
sage
lime
jade
celedon
vert
forest
olive
GREEN
teal
verdigris
citrine
chartreuse
fern
emerald
leaf
parakeet
pine
celery
lettuce
neon
sea-green
laurel
viridian
shamrock
myrtle
malachite
jungle
juniper
turquoise
avocado
mint
harlequin

rhubarb
ochre
beet
Sedona
crimson
mahogany
bordeaux
cardinal
pomegranate
salmon
rouge
cerise
brick
merlot
raspberry
hibiscus
ruby
PINK
RED
claret
pimento
candy
fuchsia
mulberry
chili
amaranth
cinnamon
strawberry
terra-cotta
vermilion
garnet
cranberry
shiraz
carmine
scarlet
paprika
puce
barn maroon
sangria
fire-engine
copper
cherry
poppy
burgundy
cabernet
coral
rose
tobasco
ginger
bacon
bubblegum
magenta
rust
salsa
cayenne
apple

goldenrod
banana
schoolbus
dandelion
flaxen
apricot
butter
vanilla
blonde
lemon
Tuscan
gold
citrine
pineapple
maize
lion
aureolin
marigold
YELLOW
ochre
butterscotch
saffron
beige
sunflower
custard
amber
canary
honey
daffodil
buff
fire
chiffon
straw
dijon
jonquil
cream
mustard
corn
jasmine

cyan
light tiffany
midnight cerulean
cadet periwinkle
capri turquoise azure violet-blue robin's
peacock cobalt steel lapis sky indigo ocean
teal navy BLUE baby cornflower
aqua ultramarine
blue-gray alice lazuli blue-green
powder royal sapphire hice
viridian
heather slate

coconut snow
cauliflower
lace
chiffon
seashell
frost
smoke
alabaster
milky
ties ecru
honeydew
powder
daisy
lily-white
WHITE
pearly
dove
ghostwhite
linen
porcelain
cotton
ivory
parchment
powdery
sugar
creamy
marble
eggshell
bone
champagne
cream
pasty

ink
ebony
soot
night
onyx
raven
BLACK
obsidian
crow-black
pitch
sable
coal
peppercorn

bombastic silvery breathy reedy cold thin steady dead fruity spooky
penetrating tight wistful velvety airy thick scratchy parched
croaky musical gravelly guttural strident quiet nasal taut light nervous pleasant racous strangled disembodied honeyed
soft gruff flat
loud deep
unpleasant dumb matter-of-fact hoarse annoying dry brittle sexy tremulous grating
monotonous wheezy appealing orotund pitched throaty plummy
high-pitched clear abrasive pompous wobbly
husky ringing small low shrill
singsong smoky rough

sizzling
spongy
feverish
pointy
throb
bristly
pulpy
bloom
glassy
cushiony
thorny
feathery
prickly
hair
gritty
pithy
velvety
wobbly
barbed
horned
parched
strong
sandy
powdery
mushy
tufted
glacial
itch
energizing
smooth
scalding
stiff
electirfying
slippery
thin
splintery
hairy
rough
coarse
fiery
arctic
blazing
slick
freezing
warm
flexible
fluid
stale
stagnant
hot
broiling
prickling
elastic
muggy
cold
scratchy
flaming
airy
blistering
stuffy
silen
pliable
creamy
soft
silky
burning
even
grainy
nippy
stirring
dry
roasting
rigid
staring
hard
jagged
fluffy
cool
crumbly
sharp
supple
malleable
raising
springy
abrasive
suffocating
frictionless
delicate
lumpy
breezy
stainy
serrated
rubbery
gelatinousy
arousing
frosty
furry
leafy
rumpled
tingly
doughy
porous
uniform
spiked
cottony
flabby
fetid
fleshy
flush
calm
dusty
humid
limpid
firm

Tip: Break out your thesaurus and find the precise word you need!

Hear Well Went
Suddenly Need
Great
Shrug Just Grin
Pretty Nod
Bad Literally Imagine Try
Watch Very Smile

LAZY WORDS

Gaze
Good See Really Sigh
Walk Like sit Almost
-LY Remember
Know Realize Breathe Get
Stand Wonder Since
Feel Look Seem

Writerly Resources

Advice and assistance on:

- Creativity
- Writing
- Editing
- Publishing
- Marketing
- Handy Worksheets
- Tracking Tools

"Beware of advice — even this."
— Carl Sandburg

Creativity

Creative Play: A Guide for the Artistic Path by award winning author Michele Venné, gives writers proven techniques for tapping into their creative side.

Be sure to have a copy of Damon Suede's *Verbalize* on hand to create true-to-life compelling characters and keep your story coherent.

A couple of must-haves for your library are Julie Cameron's *The Artist's Way* and Stephen Pressfield's *The War of Art.*

Another great reference for creativity is, *What If? Writing Exercises for Fiction Writers* by Anne Bernays and Pamela Painter.

Also, go to *The Story Starter* at http://thestorystarter.com/ and check out their story idea generator.

Visit the *Creativity Portal* for prompts and hundreds of unique ideas for stories and other creative projects. http://creativity-portal.com/

Never fear the blank page again when you click on either Tumbler or Reddit for more writing prompts and inspiration than you can possibly handle: http://writingprompts.tumblr.com/ and https://reddit.com/r/WritingPrompts/

Try a bit of advice from successful authors on how they become (and stay) inspired to put pen to page. https://thejohnfox.com/2016/06/writing-inspiration/

Writing

> *"One thing that helps is to give myself permission to write badly. I tell myself that I'm going to do my 5 or 10 pages no matter what, and that I can always tear them up the following morning if I want. I'll have lost nothing...writing and tearing up 5 pages would leave me no further behind than if I took the day off."*
>
> -Lawrence Block

Kris Tualla's *A Primer for Beginning Authors* gives great advice for anyone considering a career in writing fiction.

For serious writers of all levels, here are a few more necessities for your library shelf:

Alan Black's *How To Start, Write, and Finish Your First Novel*

Stephen King's *On Writing*

Anne Lamott's *Bird by Bird*

Larry Brooks's *Story Engineering and Story Physics*

Blake Snyder's *Save the Cat*

Roy Peter Clark's *Writing Tools: 55 Essential Strategies for Every Writer*

If you prefer to speak your story instead of typing it, you'll want to try Dragon Naturally Speaking by http://Nuance.com. There's almost always a coupon offered online, so be sure to look for it. Please note: if you take the time to properly train Dragon, you won't need to do too much editing.

Current, quality information for writers is available at http://WritersMarket.com. Plus they have a wonderful selection of books for writers.

Editing

> *"I know now that when a man finishes some important task, like writing a book, when the last word is written he wants to start over and do the job right."*
>
> -James Michener

Here's a bonus quote for your critique partners and beta-readers…

> *"Where were you fellows when the paper was blank?"*
>
> -Fred Allen

Because there is almost always a more interesting way to say something, try reading and exploring with the book *Word Magic* by Cindy Rogers during the rewriting and editing process.

Find the perfect word using the *Random House Word Menu* by Stephen Glazier, *Describer's Dictionary* by David Grambs, and the *Synonym Finder* by Rodale.

For impeccable grammar try *Eats, Shoots & Leaves* by Lynne Truss, *The Glamour of Grammar* by Roy Peter Clark, and *Grammar Girl's Quick and Dirty Tips* by Mignon Fogarty.

Strunk & White's *Elements of Style* and *The Chicago Manual of Style* (either the book or online subscription service) are both necessary for professional writers.

Strategic Rewriting by yours truly, Anna Questerly, gives writers advice they can use to make their editing and rewriting process easier.

Aside from word processors, online editors are probably the handiest thing ever invented for writers. Check out http://Grammarly.com, or the Hemingboard app on your smartphone, and learn how to get the most out of Microsoft Word by visiting this website: https://makeuseof.com/tag/x-ways-spell-grammar-check-microsoft-word-using-different-dictionaries-languages/

Publishing

> *"Publication is a marathon, not a sprint.*
> *Writing the book is only the start."*
>
> - Jo Linsdell

Yes, you need to get a copyright! Before you publish your work, protect it. Learn how with *Protect Your Writings* by Intellectual Rights Attorney, Maria Crimi Speth.

Find reputable publishers and agents with the *Writer's Market 2018: The Most Trusted Guide to Getting Published* and *Guide to Literary Agents 2018: The Most Trusted Guide to Getting Published*.

If you are planning to submit to literary agents, be sure to check out http://AgentQuery.com, and use our handy-dandy tracking sheet on page 149.

Double check for swindlers and scammers with http://WriterBeware.com and the possibly-soon-to-be-relaunched predators & editors site at http://abosolutewrite.com/

Learning from other writers is key. If you're self-publishing, be sure to hit the forums on Smashwords, Amazon's CreateSpace, and KDP online publishing.

For information on formatting, visit https://selfpublishingadvice.org and/or read *How to Format Your Book in Word* by Colin Dunbar and Bronson Dunbar.

For gorgeous, affordable covers, try http://TheCoverCollection.com/ or to create your own, check out https://kindlepreneur.com/book-cover-design/

To find editors and proofreaders, cover designers, formatters, and illustrators for hire, try http://Fiverr.com (Make sure to read the reviews.)

Marketing

"The freelance writer is a man who is paid per piece or per word or perhaps."

-Robert Benchely

Becoming an Authorpreneur by Kris Tualla is a great place to start your marketing adventure.

You will find *Social Media for Authors* by Laura Orsini to be helpful, too.

If you're not sure where to begin your marketing journey, this Choose-Your-Own-Adventure style ebook will become indispensable: *Your A Game: winning promo for genre fiction* by Damon Suede and Heidi Cullinan.

http://Partners.BookBub.com/ and https://advertising.amazon.com/lp/authors is Amazon's website for advertising Kindle books.

Use the Merchant Words website at http://MerchantWords.com/ to find keywords and long-tail key words for online advertising. Make sure to search for their coupon.

http://Banners.com makes professional and affordable banners for signing events. Order a banner 60 inches by 30 inches. Design the bottom 30 inches to reflect your brand. It will drape over the front of the table. Keep the top 30 inches a muted or solid color to use as a table cover and back drop to showcase your books.

Another book to check out is *Book Marketing is Dead: Book Promotion Secrets You MUST Know BEFORE You Publish* by Derek Murphy.

There are also a few blogs writers find helpful in marketing. When you get a chance check these out:

https://yourwriterplatform.com/promote-and-market-your-book/
https://insights.bookbub.com/book-marketing-ideas/

Marketing Notes

Genre:

Author Name:

Target Reader:

Possible Key Words:

Local/Regional Events and Dates:

Local Bookstores & Libraries

Company Name: Contact:
Email: Phone:
Address:
Will they: Order Books   Buy Books   Offer Consignment   Host Signings/Events
Notes:

Company Name: Contact:
Email: Phone:
Address:
Will they: Order Books   Buy Books   Offer Consignment   Host Signings/Events
Notes:

Company Name: Contact:
Email: Phone:
Address:
Will they: Order Books   Buy Books   Offer Consignment   Host Signings/Events
Notes:

Company Name: Contact:
Email: Phone:
Address:
Will they: Order Books   Buy Books   Offer Consignment   Host Signings/Events
Notes:

Company Name: Contact:
Email: Phone:
Address:
Will they: Order Books   Buy Books   Offer Consignment   Host Signings/Events
Notes:

Company Name: Contact:
Email: Phone:
Address:
Will they: Order Books   Buy Books   Offer Consignment   Host Signings/Events
Notes:

Company Name: Contact:
Email: Phone:
Address:
Will they: Order Books   Buy Books   Offer Consignment   Host Signings/Events
Notes:

Company Name: Contact:
Email: Phone:
Address:
Will they: Order Books   Buy Books   Offer Consignment   Host Signings/Events
Notes:

Company Name: Contact:
Email: Phone:
Address:
Will they: Order Books   Buy Books   Offer Consignment   Host Signings/Events
Notes:

Company Name: Contact:
Email: Phone:
Address:
Will they: Order Books   Buy Books   Offer Consignment   Host Signings/Events
Notes:

Company Name: Contact:
Email: Phone:
Address:
Will they: Order Books   Buy Books   Offer Consignment   Host Signings/Events
Notes:

Company Name: Contact:
Email: Phone:
Address:
Will they: Order Books   Buy Books   Offer Consignment   Host Signings/Events
Notes:

Proofreading Tips

Although there are ways the computer can help with proofreading, instead of working from a computer screen, print out at least one of your read-throughs.

Check separately for each kind of error, and move from the most to the least important. For example: spelling, homonyms, punctuation, grammar, etc.

Read your work backwards, sentence by sentence, and then read it again forwards to make sure your subjects and verbs agree. Or hide the next row using a blank sheet of paper or index card. These techniques keep you from skipping ahead and getting lost in the story and missing mistakes.

Read out loud. It's much easier to spot run-on sentences and flip-flopped words. You'll also hear other problems you may not see when reading silently, like missing or extra words. If possible, have someone else read aloud while you sit at your screen, reading along and making changes as needed.

Use the search or find/replace function in your word processing program to find mistakes you're likely to make. For example, if you learned to type using two spaces after a period and can't seem to break the habit, type two blank spaces in **find** and one blank space in **replace** and select **replace all** to fix it quickly. *Note: Be careful using the* **replace all** *function too often. Best practice is to save your work just prior to using it.*

There, their, they're...don't despair — you can also use the find function to search for homonyms.

End with a spelling check, using your spell checker. Also try software for writers such as Grammarly or HemingwayApp. Remember that a spell checker won't catch mistakes with homonyms (e.g., rains, reigns, reins) or certain typos (like 'he' for 'she').

You will most likely need to read your work a dozen times or more prior to publication. Many new writers feel "it's good enough" and doesn't need to be perfect — trust me, it won't be perfect even if your read it twenty times. They almost always end up pulling their work down later to rewrite it because of nasty reviews. Try to be patient; it won't be perfect, but get it as close as you can. You won't regret it.

Proofreader's Marks

Standardization of marks help writers clearly communicate with the rest of their editorial team.

℘	Delete character, word, or sentence	∧	Insert character, word, or sentence
⌒	Delete Space	#	Insert Space
(stet)	Let it Stand	⋏	Insert Comma
¶	New Paragraph	⋎	Insert Apostrophe
]	Move Right	⋎⋎	Insert Quotation Marks
[	Move Left	⊙	Insert Period
][	Center	?	Insert Question Mark
(ital)	Italics	M̲	Insert em dash
(bf)	Bold	N̲	Insert en dash
(lc)	Lowercase	⸗	Insert hyphen
(caps)	Capitalize	(⁄)	Insert parentheses
(wf)	Wrong Font	‖	Align Vertically
⊓	Move Up	⸗	Align Horizontally
⊔	Move Down	sp	Spelling
∿	Transpose		

Font Style: Font Size:
Don't forget to embed your fonts!

Paragraphs: ☐ Indent   ☐ Block

Book Size:

Margins:

Top: Bottom:

Inside: Outside:

Style Guide Used:

Made-up and unorthodox words (spelling and definition)

Serial Comma: ☐ Yes   ☐ No

Commonly misspelled/misused
words:

Made up holidays and events:

Acronyms Used:

Goal Setting & Word Counts

WCGM (Word Count Goal for this Manuscript): _________

EDC (Estimated Days to Completion of First Draft) ______

$\textbf{WCGM} \div \textbf{EDC} = \textbf{WPD}$ (Words Needed Per Day to Reach Goal) ______

WPM (Your Average Words Written per Minute): ______

DTDW (Daily Time Dedicated to Writing): ______

$\textbf{WPD} \div \textbf{WPM} = \textbf{DWG}$ (Daily Writing Goal): ______

Sample Word Counts of Popular Books

War and Peace 587,287

Remembrance Rock 530,030

Gone with the Wind 418,053

The Fountainhead 311,596

Jonathan Strange & Mr. Norrell 308,931

Memoirs of a Geisha 186,418

Jane Eyre 183,858

Catch-22 174,269

Watership Down 156,154

The Time Traveler's Wife 155,717

Schindler's List 134,710

Sense and Sensibility 126,194

The Hobbit 95,022

The Picture of Dorian Gray 78,462

Harry Potter and the Sorcerer's Stone 77,325

Treasure Island 66,950

Brave New World 63,766

The Great Gatsby 47,094

Fahrenheit 451 46,118

Charlie and the Chocolate Factory 30,644

The Mouse and the Motorcycle 22,416

Industry Standard Word Counts by Type

Novel: 40,000 - 125,000 (depending on genre)

Novella: 17,501 - 40,000

Novelette: 7,501 - 17,500

Short Stories: 1,001 - 7,500

Flash Fiction: 100 - 1,000

Industry Standard Word Count By Genre

Non-Fiction: 70,000 - 110,000

Literary / Commercial / Women's Fiction: 80,000 - 110,000

Romance: 40,000 - 100,000

    Series Romance (Harlequin/Regency/Inspirational): 40,000 - 60,000

    Historical Romance: 75,000-100,000

Mysteries / Thrillers / Suspense: 70,000 - 100,000

    Cozy Mysteries: 70,000 -75,000

Fantasy: 90,000 - 100,000

Paranormal: 75,000 - 95,000

Horror: 80,000 - 100,000

Science-Fiction: 90,000 - 125,000

Historical: 100,000 - 120,000

New Adult Fiction: 60,000 - 85,000

Young Adult Fiction (YA): 50,000 - 80,000

Children's Fiction: 500 - 40,000

    Middle Grade: 25,000 - 40,000

    Chapter Books: 5,000 - 15,000

    Picture Books: 500 - 700

Power Words

Record the best
words to use as key
words in your
marketing materials
and for your title &
back cover copy!

Submission Tracker

Track your contest entries and submissions to agents and publishers below.

Date:	Submitted to:	Outcome:

Beta-Readers & Critique Partners Submission Tracker

Know who has your work – track your submissions to beta-readers, editors, critique partners, proofreaders, and formatters below. **Pro tip:** Use to recall who to acknowledge for their help.

Date:	Submitted to:	Due Back:

Progress	Saturday	Friday	Thursday	Wednesday	Tuesday	Monday	Sunday
Words this Week / Goal							
Words this Week / Goal							
Words this Week / Goal							
Words this Week / Goal							
Words this Month / Goal							

Progress	Saturday	Friday	Thursday	Wednesday	Tuesday	Monday	Sunday
Words this Week / Goal							
Words this Week / Goal							
Words this Week / Goal							
Words this Week / Goal							
Words this Month / Goal							

Progress	Words this Week	Goal	Words this Week	Goal	Words this Week	Goal	Words this Week	Goal	Words this Month	Goal
Saturday										
Friday										
Thursday										
Wednesday										
Tuesday										
Monday										
Sunday										

Progress — Words this Week / Goal — Words this Week / Goal — Words this Week / Goal — Words this Week / Goal — Words this Month / Goal

Saturday
Friday
Thursday
Wednesday
Tuesday
Monday
Sunday

	Sunday	Monday	Tuesday	Wednesday	Thursday	Friday	Saturday	Progress
								Words this Week / Goal
								Words this Week / Goal
								Words this Week / Goal
								Words this Week / Goal
								Words this Month / Goal

Sunday	Monday	Tuesday	Wednesday	Thursday	Friday	Saturday	Progress
							Words this Week Goal:
							Words this Week Goal:
							Words this Week Goal:
							Words this Week Goal:
							Words this Month Goal:

Progress	Saturday	Friday	Thursday	Wednesday	Tuesday	Monday	Sunday
Words this Week / Goal							
Words this Week / Goal							
Words this Week / Goal							
Words this Week / Goal							
Words this Month / Goal							

Progress	Saturday	Friday	Thursday	Wednesday	Tuesday	Monday	Sunday
Words this Week / Goal							
Words this Week / Goal							
Words this Week / Goal							
Words this Week / Goal							
Words this Month / Goal							

Sunday	Monday	Tuesday	Wednesday	Thursday	Friday	Saturday	Progress
							Words this Week Goal
							Words this Week Goal
							Words this Week Goal
							Words this Week Goal
							Words this Month Goal

Progress	Saturday	Friday	Thursday	Wednesday	Tuesday	Monday	Sunday
Words this Week / Goal							
Words this Week / Goal							
Words this Week / Goal							
Words this Week / Goal							
Words this Month / Goal							

Progress	Words this Week / Goal	Words this Week / Goal	Words this Week / Goal	Words this Week / Goal	Words this Month / Goal
Saturday					
Friday					
Thursday					
Wednesday					
Tuesday					
Monday					
Sunday					

Progress	Saturday	Friday	Thursday	Wednesday	Tuesday	Monday	Sunday
Words this Week / Goal							
Words this Week / Goal							
Words this Week / Goal							
Words this Week / Goal							
Words this Month / Goal							

Your Notes

Notes:

Notes:

Notes:

Self Publishing Checklist

☐ Narration completed for Audio Book
☐ Format eBooks
☐ Proof Review (Repeat As Necessary)

Business

☐ Set up LLC
☐ Choose Intellectual Rights & Estate Planning Attorneys
☐ Checking Account
☐ File for Copyright
☐ File for any needed permissions/agreements
☐ Purchase ISBN and Barcode
☐ Setup Accounts with
   ○ Createspace
   ○ Audible
   ○ Kindle
   ○ Smashwords
   ○ iTunes
   ○ Barnes & Noble

Writing

☐ First Draft
☐ Title
☐ Title Page
☐ Copyright Page
☐ Foreword
☐ Acknowledgements
☐ Table of Contents (if needed)
☐ Index (if needed)
☐ Pen Name (if desired)
☐ Your Bio
☐ Elevator Pitch & Tagline
☐ Back Cover Text

Editing

☐ Structural Editing
☐ Fact Checking/Research
☐ Beta Readers
☐ Critique Group
☐ Polishing
☐ Copy Editing
☐ Proofreading (Repeat As Necessary)

Marketing

☐ Target Audience
☐ Establish Pricing for Each Format
☐ Set Release Date
☐ Set up Preorder Sales
☐ Reviews
☐ Plan Release Party
☐ Set up Signing Opportunities
☐ Set up Interview/Blog Tours
☐ Build a Social Media Platform
☐ Your Photograph
☐ Create Author Pages on Amazon Central/Smashwords/Audible
☐ Design Website
☐ Email List
☐ Social Media Accounts

Publishing

☐ Formatting
☐ List previous or planned books in current work
☐ Cover Design
☐ eBook

Other Books and Projects by Anna Questerly

Available Online & in Bookstores

A fun collection of short stories.

Pangaea, a utopian fantasy, written as A.J. Questerly

A reference guide for those new to essential oils, written as The Alchemist's Guild

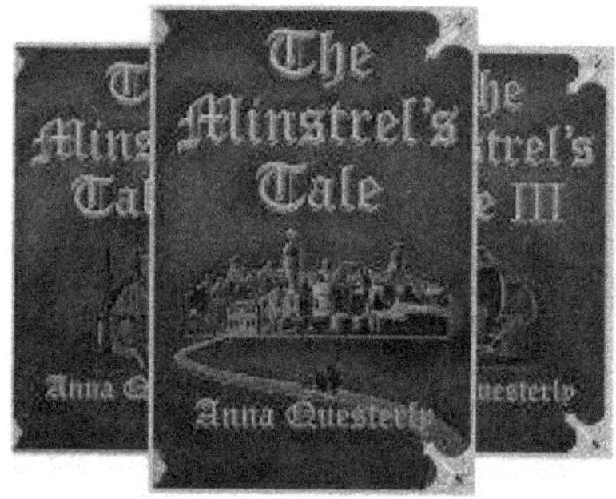

The Minstrel's Tale Trilogy

A fun, family read, filled with original fairy tales that the minstrel tells while he's on his own adventure in 14th century Europe.

Individual fairy tales from The Minstrel's Tale!

A great selection of lined journals with page numbers and a fill-in-the-blank table of contents so you can find your best ideas.

Search for Anna Questerly Journals online.

Comfortable Classics Collection

Easier-to-read editions of classic works. Perfect for students of classical literature and great to collect!

Visit www.comfortableclassics.com/ for individual titles.

A resource for writers!